Greater Than a Tourist Madrid Spain

50 Travel Tips from a Local

Ana Alonso

Order Information: To order this title please email lbrenenc@gmail.com or visit GreaterThanATourist.com. A bulk discount can be provided.

Cover Template Creator: Lisa Rusczyk Ed. D. using Canva.
Cover Creator: Lisa Rusczyk Ed. D.
Image: https://pixabay.com/en/madrid-monument-puerta-de-alcal%C3%A1-2179954/

Lock Haven, PA
All rights reserved.
ISBN: 9781549837340

>TOURIST

Ana Alonso

BOOK DESCRIPTION

Are you excited about planning your next trip?

Do you want to try something new?

Would you like some guidance from a local?

If you answered yes to any of these questions, then this Greater Than a Tourist book is for you.

Greater Than a Tourist by Ana Alonso offers the inside scoop on Madrid. Most travel books tell you how to sightsee. Although there's nothing wrong with that, as a part of the Greater than a Tourist series, this book will give you tips from someone who lives at your next travel destination. In these pages, you'll discover local advice that will help you throughout your trip.

Travel like a local. Slow down and get to know the people and the culture of a place. By the time you finish this book, you will be eager and prepared to travel to your next destination.

Ana Alonso

TABLE OF CONTENTS

13. Madrid Loves Soccer

14. Visit Madrid's Zero Kilometre

15. Have Some Churros For Breakfast

16. Eat A Typical Spanish Tortilla

17. Eat A Bocadillo de Calamares

18. Celebrate San Isidro

19. If You Are an Animal Lover

21. Bike Around Madrid

22. Eat and Party 24/7

23. On NYE, Go To Plaza Mayor

24. Places With A View

25. Buy A Silly Hat At A Christmas Market

26. Get Something Funky At Rastro Market

27. Get Scared At The Wax Museum

28. Go To A Market, Or Two

29. Madrid's Beer is Awesome

30. Visit The Parks

31. The Tallest Skyscraper In Spain

32. Some Strange Places In Madrid

33. Party Like A Local

DEDICATION

This book is dedicated to my family: my husband Alberto who loves to eat all places in Madrid, and my little Adrián, who loves to explore this city inch by inch, bite by bite, walking or bicycling with me. What can I say, we love to eat!

Ana Alonso

ABOUT THE AUTHOR

Ana Alonso is an entrepreneur and businesswomen that moved to Madrid in 2002 when she started living with her boyfriend there (which is now our family home) moving from the outskirts of Madrid.

Since then I have explored Madrid as much as I can, as it is a city with very old and also lots of new things.

Food excites me and this what guides my travels most of the time. Sometimes I visit a place just because I want to try food from there!

Ana Alonso

HOW TO USE THIS BOOK

The Greater Than a Tourist book series was written by someone who has lived in an area for over three months. The goal of this book is to help travelers either dream or experience different locations by providing opinions from a local. The author has made suggestions based on their own experiences. Please do your own research before traveling to the area in case the suggested places are unavailable.

Ana Alonso

FROM THE PUBLISHER

Traveling can be one of the most important parts of a person's life. The anticipation and memories that you have are some of the best. As a publisher of the Greater Than a Tourist book series, as well as the popular 50 Things to Know book series, we strive to help you learn about new places, spark your imagination, and inspire you. Wherever you are and whatever you do I wish you safe, fun, and inspiring travel.

Lisa Rusczyk Ed. D.

CZYK Publishing

Ana Alonso

WELCOME TO > TOURIST

Ana Alonso

INTRODUCTION

Madrid is an astonishing city. It is old and very modern at the same time.

We have Royal Palaces and renowned museums thanks to the Austria and Borbon dynasty.

We also have skyscrapers and bullet trains, long green parks and beltways around the city.

I think that Madrid has the best food, ambiance, and people.

I hope that with this book you decide the same and visit us!

Ana Alonso

1. When To Come

Madrid has a continental type of weather, meaning that winters are quite cold, and summers, very hot.

The best time would be during spring and autumn, as the temperature is mild (around 20°C) and it rarely rains around the year.

At winter, it gets quite cold (but never below 0°C), but it is always sunny. And in August, the 'official' vacation month, it is scorching (around 38-40°C), but there will be practically no souls around so you can have the city for yourself.

2. Bring Your Sunscreen

If you come to Madrid, don't worry about umbrellas. It almost rarely rains here (it rains two or three times a year).

But if it does, it can be a 3-day storm or five minutes. If it rains a lot in a little time, beware as everything gets flooded. Sometimes the Metro subway has to stop and traffic also stops too.

But most of the time there is a lot of sun so bring your sunscreen, and enjoy your trip!

3. Getting To Madrid

Almost all people will arrive by plane. This will mean you will

arrive at Adolfo Suarez Madrid Barajas Airport.

The fastest and easiest way to get to the center is by train or

subway. Both have connections to both terminals, so get informed

beforehand or ask at the entrance.

If you intend to buy a ticket and it says something else than MAD

(Madrid), it is probably taking you to another airport or station that

is NOT in Madrid as there is no other airport or stations. So be

careful, as going to a secondary station and then taking

transportation to Madrid will be probably worse and much more

costly than the going straight to Madrid.

4. There Are Many Ways Of Transportation

Madrid is so beautiful that you could just walk it from end to end just looking around you.

But it also has one of the best transportation systems. We have the train, subway and buses available all around the city.

The train is the most reliable. Timetables are posted online, and there is a poster at every station. And they stick to it. You can reach one end to the other of Madrid this way. Recently a Sol station was opened so you can travel fast to outer parts of the city.

The subway reaches almost everywhere, but sometimes you have to make a few line changes. Tip: unless you only have to do one ride, get the ten ride pass. For one ticket rides there is a select origin and destination for each ticket and extra stations add up to the price, so, just get one for your family and friends, and you're ready. Also, this pass works for the bus too. So, win-win!

The bus will get you anywhere. And it works 24/7. Night lines (búhos) have smaller trajectories but are useful the same and this way you will avoid hefty taxi prices.

5. Packing For Madrid

Madrid does not have a lot of extreme weather, so clothes-wise you just have to worry to wear layers so you can put some on or take some off if necessary. Winters are cold, but not Arctic cold (unless you are a person that always needs a jacket), and summers are a bit hot. Don't bring an umbrella unless it's stackable. It usually does not rain here.

If you can, bring a small bag for your money, the kind you can wear under your clothes. Some areas are known for pickpocketers. By the way, if you don't want to look like a tourist, do not wear flip-flops or sandals with socks, that is a dead giveaway that you are so. Most bars will have Wi-Fi and plugs (European style) for your phone or laptop. Always try to bring water with you as the shops at the street will rip you off (as everywhere in the world, probably).

6. Beware Of Taxis

Not that everybody is the same, but if you must take a taxi ride try to be informed a bit about where you should be going and how, since sometimes they tend to go all around Madrid to make the price meter go up, and after-wise you get a hefty surprise. If this happens, tell them to give you a sheet claim and complain.

I personally use Uber/mytaxi/Cabify (who knows if they still operate in Madrid by the time you are reading this as some cities are declaring these services unconstitutional), where you can control where and how much it is going to cost.

7. Where To Stay

Madrid has a bit of everything, so it just depends on what you want. Nowadays there are a lot of apartments available on Airbnb for rent, which makes you feel more like home, and it is what I would do.

If not, there are super fancy hotels like The Ritz and The Palace that are in the center near the Prado Museum (actually, one is in front of the other).

And if you are on a budget, and want a hotel I would recommend going a little bit further away from the absolute center (Sol) as maybe Nuevos Ministerios or Plaza Castilla area, where you can catch a train ride and go straight to the center.

But try not to stay around the airport, any train/subway ride or even the car will take at least 20-30 minutes to reach anywhere near the center.

8. Where To Go Food Shopping

Even though you are on vacation, sometimes you just need to get some shower gel, or you want some fruit or snacks for your travel. The most affordable options are Mercadona and Carrefour (which are all around Madrid). If not, you can always go to El Corte Inglés and pay a bit more.

If you want the authentic Spanish experience, try to go to a local market, like Mercado de la Cebada in La Latina or Mercado de Chamartín (metro Colombia) or Mercado Barceló. There they have stalls for each type of food, and you can get fresh, local and in-season produce.

21

9. Catch A Glimpse of Madrid's History

Madrid has been the capital for more than five centuries. Many Royal families have lived here, and still do. There has been Muslim, Christians and almost everything in between conquering and living in this city.

Probably the most important historical date is May 2, 1808, during the Independence War of Spain. Napoleon had subtly conquered many cities in the North of Spain like Barcelona and Pamplona and had the Kings secluded in Bayonne (France). The people of Madrid, as they realized that they were being taken over on that day, seeing that the French army was apprehending the rest of the Royal Family and taking them away from the Royal Palace. A giant revolt started, and the fight lasted for hours, spreading around all the city.

It did not do much, as the next day many were shot and many

22

civilians died.

Both of these days are represented by one of Spain's most famous painter: Francisco Goya, with the paintings of "El dos de mayo de 1808 en Madrid" and "El tres de mayo de 1808 en Madrid", which can be seen at Prado Museum. There are a series of paintings by Goya that represent this war, and when you see them, you can feel the sadness and the intensity of them all.

10. Go to Madrid's Beach In The Summer

If you have an itch for water, we have a 'beach' in the center, as the nearest beach is almost 350 km away. It is in Madrid Rio park near Manzanares river. It is NOT a sand beach though as it is an urban beach, so it is a giant fountain that squirts water from the floor, and has multiple shower mists.

It is ideal for a moment of disconnection and for kids that sometimes just need to get soaked in the summer and run around a bit to get tired. It also has deck chairs if you want to catch some sun.

It gets a bit crowded but it is enjoyable, just try to get there a little early or around noon (2-4 PM) as its local's lunch time.

11. Art In Every Direction

We can't talk about Madrid and not talk about Museums and Art Galleries. The oldest Gallery is Galería Kreisler that opened in 1965 on Hermosilla, 8.

If you love Modernist art, please go to Reina Sofia, where you can see many Spanish artists like Dali and Picasso. Do not miss the Guernica by Picasso. While you look at the painting, you can actually feel the anguish of the people of Guernica during the war.

And for Romanticism, Gothic and Baroque go to Prado Museum. You can see Madrid's history through the painters' eyes, as most of them were painters for the Royal Court.

Ana Alonso

"To go to bed at night in Madrid marks

you like a little queer. For a long time

your friends will be a little uncomfortable

about it. Nobody goes to bed in Madrid

until they have killed the night.

Appointments with a friend are habitually

made for after midnight at the cafe."

- Ernest Hemingway, Death in the

Afternoon

Ana Alonso

12. Kids Sometimes Need a Break

If you are traveling with your little ones, Madrid has a few spaces for a non-artsy-museum morning.

Zoo de Madrid is in Casa de Campo and has quite a few animals, including pandas, an aquarium and much more. It also has a dolphin and a bird show.

Then we have Faunia, which is a bit fancier (also in the price, too). It is smaller than the zoo, but it has a penguin area which is very cool and entertaining, it is better organized than the Zoo and kids have more activities to do.

Both of them are perfect for a quiet morning.

13. Madrid Loves Soccer

Soccer is a national sport. Madrid has three soccer teams, Real Madrid, Atlético de Madrid and Rayo Vallecano. The first two of them are in the First division and the other, in Second division. The rivalry between the teams is real, and against Barcelona, too.

When there is a match, the city stops. So if you enjoy soccer, go to a local bar and grab a beer and watch the game. If you don't, make it up for the uncrowded places!

If Real Madrid wins a major match, the Cibeles fountain will be crowded. And if Atletico wins, Neptuno fountain will be the one. People take soccer very seriously so never tease about their team; it will probably get you in trouble!

14. Visit Madrid's Zero Kilometre

The Statue of the Bear and the Strawberry Tree, or as we call it, la Estatua del Oso y el Madroño, is where Kilometro Cero is. This is the point from which the distances are measured in Spain.

The statue represents Madrid's hierarchical symbol (it's on our flag), and it was put in Plaza de Sol in 1967.

If you can try to get a picture, but it usually gets busy as tourists use it as a photo stop and Madrilenians as meeting point!

15. Have Some Churros For Breakfast

Eat churros. These are NOT the Mexican kind they sell in

Disneyland. Have it with a nice cup of chocolate.

You can go to the most typical place in Madrid, San Ginés, which

is around the center area of Sol. It is the oldest churrería place in

Madrid. It serves mostly tourists and people that get out of the

disco right next door, Joy Eslava, after a night of dancing (since

they open very early).

Or you can go to any Chocolatería Valor (there is one a few steps

away from Callao) and have excellent chocolate.

Any bar that opens early in the morning will also have churros.

Some like it to have it with café con leche. And if you feel brave,

ask for a porra, which is a thick churro (almost as a zucchini!).

16. Eat A Typical Spanish Tortilla

Madrid's best tapa is probably the Spanish tortilla, or as we call it, tortilla de patata. Again, not the Mexican tortilla. Some like it very well done, some almost liquid on the inside. Some people fight if it should have onion slices or not. But all Madrilenians will say they love tortilla.

It is the perfect mid-morning snack, and you will find it at almost any bar before lunchtime.

The best tortillas are in Juana la Loca (La Latina –Plaza Puerta de Moros), Las Tortillas de Gabino (Rafael Calvo, 10) where they have many types, and also you can go to Txirimiri (many locations in Madrid). In Estado Puro (Plaza de Neptuno) you can have a deconstructed tortilla which is very good.

17. Eat A Bocadillo de Calamares

The ONE sandwich in Madrid is the Calamari sandwich, or as we call it, bocadillo de calamares. It is a breaded calamari sandwich made with French bread. Sometimes it is served with mayonnaise, some not.

Please eat one from El Brillante which is at the Atocha area or Postas bar at Postas street, if you can, but also around Plaza Mayor you will have tons of places. Please look around for prices (at the Plaza) before you actually go in, to avoid surprises.

18. Celebrate San Isidro

San Isidro Labrador is Madrid's saint, and its festivity is on May 15. It is a big day for people here, where locals dress as chulapos and chulapas (you can see the dresses in Goya's paintings). A few days before the 15th the festivities start, from Plaza Mayor all the way to Las Vistillas (right across the river) there are concerts, theatres for kids, a parade and lots of other activities. There is also lemonade (which is NOT for kids) and rosquillas de San Isidro which are typical of this day.

So if you come around the 15th of May, check the local guides and try to do some 'madrileño' stuff.

It gets a bit crowded, but this would be the most typical thing you could do.

19. If You Are an Animal Lover

And you are in Madrid the 17th of January, visit San Anton church in Hortaleza, 63. That day, the priest of the church blesses all animals as San Antón is the patron of animals. It is a party, as a long line form and they bless any type of animal.

20. Try Madrid's Wine

Spain's most famous wine is La Rioja's. But that doesn't mean that Madrid's wines are not good. Quite the contrary.

We have many wineries, so when you go have some tapas, instead of having some sangria, try some local wine, you will not regret it.

Some of the most notorious wines are Tagonius, Tejoneras Alta Seleccion, Valquejigoso, Félix Martínez, Licinia and Marañones.

If you want you can visit some Bodegas, as Bodegas Castejón in Arganda (40 minutes away from the centre), Viñedos de El Regajar in Aranjuez, or Quebel in Pozuelo del Rey. Just check out their websites for tour information.

Es Madrid patria de todos, pues en su

mundo pequeño son hijos de igual cariño

naturales y extranjeros. 'Madrid is a

place for everybody, as in its small world

all are equally loved locals and

foreigners'.

Calderón de la Barca — El maestro de

danzar

Ana Alonso

21. Bike Around Madrid

Madrid is slowly becoming a bicycle-friendly city. Almost all of the big parks have rentals (there are many on the sides of Madrid Rio), and Retiro Park has Rent and Roll Madrid, having two locations at the entrance of the park (one on street Felipe IV, 10 and the other street Salustiano Olózaga, 14 near Puerta de Alcalá.

Most of the bigger streets around the city have a bicycle lane or a shared car/bike lane so you can move around the city swiftly and carbon free!

Trixy.com is also available around Sol/Callao at Calle Jardines, 12 where they also offer tours.
And last but not least, the app DonkeyRepublic offers many pickup sites to rent a bike all around Madrid. Now, just pedal around the city!

22. Eat and Party 24/7

Madrid is known for not having a particular hour for anything. Since European and American timings are so different, and restaurants and cafes cater to both, you can eat and drink all day long.

Breakfast, most of the time, is served from 7 am until around noon at most places. And from noon until five, lunch. After that up 'till midnight or even 1 or 2 in the morning, you can have dinner. So maybe you will be having lunch, and that will be somebody else's breakfast or dinner time!

If you are unsure about the restaurant/cafe not having the kitchen open, just ask.

Also, you can also get a drink and dance all day. Thursday is a popular day for going out amongst madrileños (we call it juernes – which is a mix of jueves and Viernes Thursday and Friday- and also, juerga which is party time), and some of them start at happy hour or an after-work special which can start around 6 or 7 pm. Then you can go to an actual bar which will be open until 2 or 3 AM. After that, discos will be open until 6. And if you are still up, you can go to an after-hours disco which is open from 6 until noon or so.

There is a new way of going out, and it is doing it in the afternoon, and we call it 'tardeo' (it would be called 'afternooning' in English, it isn't an actual word). Instead of going out at night you can go out and have some drinks in the afternoon.

So, relax and enjoy. Just go with the flow. There are not too many rules in Madrid so... just go!

23. On NYE, Go To Plaza Mayor

In Spain we have a tradition where we eat 12 grapes, 'the grapes of luck' or 'uvas de la suerte' right before the New Year starts.

People go to Plaza Mayor to watch the clock dong 12 times, and eat one grape on each one, hopefully finishing before the new year starts.

This is actually shown on television, and people follow the clock from home. It's the most-watched program of the year.

If you don't want to go on the 31st and avoid super crowds, you can do it while they test the clock, which they do on the 30th at noon and midnight, and the 31st at noon.

24. Places With A View

Madrid has quite an astonishing cityscape, as the mixture of old and new makes it a fascinating view.

Many hotels have a terrace, and some fancy bars too. Hotel Urban has one of the poshest bars in a terrace in Madrid.

And out of a hotel, the most famous terrace is the Círculo de Bellas Artes, where you can see all the center of Madrid. If you go, please do so before 8 PM.

If you want a change of style, go to Templo de Debod near Plaza España where you can watch the sunset surrounded by an Egyptian temple.

Madrid also has a cableway, the Teleférico. It takes you from Parque de Rosales all the way up to Casa de Campo. You can get on it at the top or on the bottom, and get off and go for a walk if you get the round-trip ticket.

43

Ana Alonso

Also, the looks from Faro de Moncloa are precious since you can see practically all Madrid (the Royal Palace, Cibeles, the Cathedral, Gran Vía street…).

At the Almudena Cathedral, which is astonishing by itself (King Felipe got married there) you can also go all the way to the top and see all the surroundings. But this ticket will cost you 6 euros.

And right next door you can see the south of Madrid from the gardens of the Royal Palace.

.

25. Buy A Silly Hat At A Christmas Market

In Madrid, as in all cities, Christmas lights are turned on very soon, so it is not considered 'Christmas time' until the Market at Plaza Mayor is opened. When that happens, you will go around the city center and most of the people will be wearing goofy hats and crazy wigs, no matter the age. It's a Madrid tradition!

Also you can get Christmas decorations and get some shopping done, but most of the locals just go to get their hats & wigs.

26. Get Something Funky At Rastro Market

The Rastro Market is probably the most famous thing to do on Sunday mornings in Madrid. Because of the shopping and also because the liveliness around it.

If you are in the mood for shopping, you should be aware that there are some specialized areas: the bird street at Fray Ceferino Perez

45

St. The painter street at San Cayetano St. Games – cards and other collectibles around Rodas street and Plaza General Vara del rey. And last but not least, old books around Carnero.

Also there are lots of antique and art shops, if that's your thing, who knows if you will find a treasure!

If you do stop to shop PLEASE be careful with your belongings. Here there are very skilled pickpockets around so beware.

 People take their time to have a little tapa and a beer before lunch at the bars around the area. One of the most famous bars is Casa Amadeo Los Caracoles (at the Plaza del Cascorro) where the specialty is snails. If you want a typical Madrilenian soup, our Cocido Madrileño, go to Malacatín (Ruda, 5). If you like boquerones en vinagre (marinated anchovies – which are a delicacy!), go to Cervecería Arganzuela at Arganzuela, 3.

27. Get Scared At The Wax Museum

Madrid has a very freaky Wax Museum, at Paseo de Recoletos, 41.

This is not Madame Tussauds but still worth the visit.

Most of the wax figures are good, but some are noticeably bad, but

it makes a nice change of pace from art, sports or shopping.

Kids will enjoy it, and adults too, as its organized by stories. So it

gives you a glimpse of Spain's history and most famous people.

The only thing is that the tour is in Spanish so if you need it to be

translated this is not your place.

28. Go To A Market, Or Two

The last few years have seen a rise in market spaces that also serve

as bars/restaurants. This is a paradise for foodies like me since it

allows you to taste many different foods in a tapas way in the same

place. There are quite a few, so here I tell you my favorites.

- San Antón (Augusto Figueroa, 26): in the center area. On top, it has a nice terrace restaurant where you can send the food you bought downstairs to make.

- San Miguel (Plaza San Miguel): probably the most touristy one. It is almost the most expensive. Also a mix of stores/bars/places to eat. But try not to go there unless you don't have time as it will be costly and very full of people. But there you can taste wine, cheese and other Spanish delicacies.

- San Fernando (Embajadores, 41). Again, with a mixture of food stalls and bars. This one is not too fancy, but you have Japanese, Mexican, Greek and many other types of food. Also beer & wine places. Excellent quality and value.

- Vallehermoso (Vallehermoso, 36). A market with quite a few restaurants/bars. It has many quality bites as Kitchen 154 and Gint (which is Gluten Free!). If you are a foodie, this market will not disappoint.

29. Madrid's Beer is Awesome

In the last few years, many breweries have started in Madrid. Again, if you can try a local beer instead of the typical Cruzcampo, Estrella Galicia or any other household Spanish brands (which are good but not from Madrid!). Mahou is from Madrid but since it's a giant national brand I don't count it as a local brewery.

The most notorious beers from Madrid are Cerveza Cibeles and Cervezas La Virgen. Both offer tours to their factories, and they are not far away from the city center. Cervezas Cibeles is in Leganés (Petroleo,34) and La Virgen Cervezas is in Las Rozas (Turin, 13). Both are excellent!

You can find them at most of bars and restaurants so just ask.

30. Visit The Parks

Madrid has quite a few green areas. The most famous one is El Buen Retiro park. This was built many years ago, and it has a lake inside it, where you can ride on a boat. It also has a few structures like Palacio de Cristal. It is right behind Prado Museum so if you go there try to check it out.

South of the city is Madrid Río park, which goes along Manzanares Río. It is a recently built park, and it has gym areas (for grownups and elderly), parks for kids and dogs and cafeterias/bars. So it is quite a nice walk, as it mixes it up with different park styles (some are trampolines, another is a climb area, another a slide... there are many different types of parks here).

"I mean, the Constitution of this country

was written 200 years ago. The house I

was living in Madrid is 350 years old!

America is still a project, and you guys

are working on it and bringing new things

to it

Antonio Banderas

Ana Alonso

31. The Tallest Skyscraper In Spain

If you like modern structures, don't miss the Four Towers Business Area. There is the tallest building in Spain, the PwC tower.

And the tower right next to it, the Eurostars Tower, has a restaurant inside (Volvoreta) so if you want to take a look above Madrid, this would be the place. A few steps away is the Kio Towers, which make an inverted V shape in the North of Madrid which makes a nice picture.

And a bit North of the four towers is the BBVA Bank headquarters, which has the shape of a candle light.

32. Some Strange Places In Madrid

Calle de Rompelanzas is Madrid's shortest street. It's less than 20 meters long. It is between Carmen and Preciados Street, right in the center of Madrid.

The narrowest street in the whole world is in Madrid, in Tetuan. It's 42 cm wide!

Madrid's narrowest building is in calle Mayor, 61. It is only 5 meters wide.

And the oldest building is Casa y Torre de los Lujanes, which is right in Madrid's center. But technically the oldest building is NOT from Madrid, but from Egypt!! The Debod Temple, was a gift to our country, and it is older than the XV century building, as it's from II BC.

33. Party Like A Local

There are quite a few bar areas in Madrid. A fancy one is in Avenida de Brazil. It is a little area with quaint little bars and restaurants. The Irish Rover is a classic. Across Castellana Ave. is the Salamanca area, which also has lots of posh bars.

Then we have Huertas, really near Sol. Around Plaza de Santa Ana there are tons of bars, including a Hawaiian Bar, Mauna Loa.

There is also a cool place for drinking Sangría, which is las Cuevas del Sésamo. It seems a bit scary at first as you go into a cave (as its name says) but it is a lovely place!

Malasaña is the grunge/alternative area, where the students of Universities go. Siroco and Tupperware are psychedelic discos where you will just have a good time.

34. Offbeat Places In Madrid

There are quite a few places that are a bit unusual, as the

Monasterio de las Descalzas Reales, which is really near Sol. It is

+500 years old Monastery, and it is still operating, so you can't

visit it entirely, but you will not regret it.

The 11-M Monument in Atocha is for remembering the hundreds

of people dead on the attacks of 11th of March 2004.

If you like angel statues, the most famous one is at the Retiro Park,

but there is another one, less known, on the top of Milaneses, 3

with Plaza Mayor.

And if you fancy candy, there is a typical candy of Madrid, which

is the violet candy. If you wish to get some, go to La Violeta (Plaza

Canalejas, 6).

35. Practice Tai Chi With The Locals

Madrid has quite a Chinese community, and you can see it on Saturday mornings in Madrid Rio. Every Saturday there is practice around the Puente Monumental de Arganzuela (you can't miss it it's a giant spiral bridge), and you can do it for free, or just watch as it is quite spectacular.

36. Go To Matadero For Some Art & Fun

Matadero is an old matadero (a slaughterhouse) rehabilitated into an art and family space. They have areas with art expositions, and almost every weekend there is some event like a local food market, art markets, food truck weekends and such. So if you come to Madrid I invite you to come as probably there is some cool event going around.

If you want to eat something eat at the stalls but not at the bars or restaurants inside, as sometimes they are not good, go outside the Matadero to Plaza General Maroto. There is a fish place there, Marisquería O Portiño. Ask for a fish platter (they have quite a few), that comes with a Galician bottle of wine. They bring the sea to you, and it's fantastic. If you are not into fish, you can go to Costello Rio which is a family style hamburger and Tex-mex restaurant.

37. Love Cats? Go To La Gatoteca

In Madrid, we have a cat bar called La Gatoteca. It's at Argumosa, 28 near Atocha. You can go there and spend some time with the cats while you have some coffee. And if you wish, you can purchase something and help the center as they also adopt and take care of abandoned cats, so you are doing a great deed!

By the way, did you know that they call people from Madrid gatos (cats)? In 1085 (when Madrid was taken over by Muslims and even though Spaniards tried and tried to recover the city could not) a soldier swiftly crawled up the wall helped by a dagger where their flag was up. And he managed to change it to the Christian one. People started calling him and his family 'gatos' and eventually all people that were born in Madrid were called like that.

38. Have A Burger

And we are not talking about McDonald's or Burger King here. In the last few years, the burger market has exploded, and there are many places to have a superb hamburger meal. If you are a few days here, it will probably be a nice change from all the tapas and cocidos.

I love Mad Café in La Latina (Cava Alta, 13), but try to make a reservation before you go. They have American beer and desserts. Also, you can go to any New York Burger (many locations in Madrid) to have almost any type of burger (20 styles and counting!). Last but not least, I recommend Sublime Food. It doesn't matter if you are a fitness fiend, are a vegetarian or celiac, or you just love to pork out they will have something for you (like their famous donut-burger and almost 20 varieties, or a protein bun or fitness patty), and tons of delicious desserts.

39. Go To The Oldest Restaurant In The World

It's right here, in Madrid. And it's near the center! Restaurante

Sobrino de Botín (Cuchilleros, 17) is the oldest, founded in 1725.

The artist Francisco de Goya (the one from the paintings in Prado

museum) worked there. And Ernest Hemingway talks about it in

one of his books.

This place is all about traditional Spanish food so order something

from their fire ovens like roast suckling pig or lamb, and a platter

of jamón y queso, with some vegetables (mushrooms,

asparagus...). Just let the waiter guide you, it will not disappoint.

Beware, the place is on the expensive side!

40. Get Some Genuine Madrid Leather & Clothes

Madrid is home base of one of the most famous fashion luxury brands, who's speciality is leather goods. I am talking about Loewe. Their bags and clothing have superior quality, and their biggest shop is at Serrano, 34.

If you like quirky clothes don't miss Agatha Ruiz de la Prada's items, at Serrano, 27.

Last but not least visit Felipe Varela's store, the Queen's favorite designer, at Ortega y Gasset, 30. He makes elegant and sophisticated clothes for women.

"¡Vete a freír espárragos!"

is what we say when you want that

annoying friend to go away

Ana Alonso

41. Eat Tapas In La Latina

This is quite a common tip, but I am going to expand it. Almost all places are great, but the ones right at the center are quite crowded.

Try to walk around the little streets; you will find little gems there. If you are a celiac, go to Taberna La Concha (Cava Baja, 17), their food is absolutely scrumptious.

If you go into La Cebada Market (I know it looks a bit dingy but go inside) they have little bars (even a taco place!). Some of the fish shops will cut and prepare anything for you (maybe some shrimp or a delightful crab) so you can eat it right there.

And if you want a bit of everything on just one street, go down to Calatrava street. It starts with Muñiz Bar (again, looks daunting but go in) at Calatrava, 3 and ask for whatever you fancy to drink. They will give you a generous free tapa with each drink. Then go up the street to Casa Dani (Calatrava, 11) and get some ham or cheese or maybe Cecina (like Serrano ham, but made from beef instead of pork).

After that go to Casa Gerardo (Calatrava, 21). Their selection of cheese and wines is unbelievable. And if you love pickled food, this is your place. Ask for some berenjenas (pickled eggplants) or some pickles (filled with anchovies and pepper). And after that whatever cheese you fancy with some gorgeous wine.

42. Watch the Three Kings Parade

Here Christmas is celebrated but not so much Santa Claus but the Three Kings (which are the three kings from Orient that visited Jesus after his birth bringing him three gifts, five days later).

And a tradition was built around this event, a Parade. Almost every city in Spain has it on the night of the 5th of January, Madrid's one being the biggest and fanciest.

If you want to watch it, you should go a few hours before as it gets pretty crowded. If you watch it around Cibeles, there is usually a few concerts as that is the end of the parade and it takes a few hours to go from Nuevos Ministerios to Cibeles.

As the carriages go by, they throw candy, for the delight of all the kids around. The Three Kings will appear to end the parade, finishing up the show.

43. Watch Some Zarzuela

El Teatro de La Zarzuela is a theatre where they usually sing Zarzuela, a traditional Spanish genre, and its right in the center at Jovellanos, 4.

They have theatre all year around being a feast for the ears and eyes. Sometimes they do lyrical shows and little operas, and even concerts.

Just check out their website to see what is available for that season, as some shows are for a few days and others, for a few months.

44. Chueca Is The LGBT Scene

Go to Chueca for an afternoon. You can't miss the Metro stop as its decorated on the inside with a rainbow wall.

Here you will find cool clothes shops to buy modern attire, chic restaurants and the latest food trends, bars and disco-bars...

If you love Asian food, go to Reina street where there you can find sushi places, udon restaurants and even a Teriyaki bar.

If you like sweets, go to Mama Framboise (Fernando VI, 23) a French pastry shop or La Duquesita (Fernando VI, 2), one of Madrid's oldest pastry shop. Get some roscón de reyes if its Christmas time!

45. Bravas Are For The Brave

Patatas bravas is a classic tapa in Madrid. And there is a fierce war to declare who makes the best.

Some people say it's at Docamar (Alcala, 337), but since it's quite far away from the center, probably your near Sol so go to Las Bravas (Alvarez Gato, 3) or if you are around La Latina, at La Posada del Dragon (Cava Baja, 14).

You will probably find Bravas at any tapas place, so do yourself a favor and try some. Some places can make a half platter with bravas and the other with aioli (garlic mayo) which is a totally different treat, so try not to miss that!

46. Listen to Gregorian Chants

This is not a usual thing you can do out of monasteries or churches that are far away from the city.

Well, you can go to Santa Maria Real de Monserrat church at San Bernardo, 79 (right near Gran Via) and every Sunday at noon the monks sing Gregorian chants.

So if you want to do something relaxed, please go.

47. Get Some Lottery

Madrid has quite a perch for buying lottery, especially Christmas lottery as it has the biggest prizes. Christmas lottery is sold from July to 21st of December, as the 22nd is the actual prize draw. There is a very famous place to get that lottery and its called Doña Manolita, at Carmen, 22. The lines for the lottery gets longer as Christmas approaches. Why is it famous? Because it has sold 'the golden ticket' for quite a few years, probably because it sells so much lottery.

So if you are lottery type person, maybe think about getting a lottery ticket, perhaps at Doña Manolita or maybe somewhere else…

48. In August, There Is Fiesta All Around

If you are brave enough to come in August, visit the local fiestas. From the beginning until the end of August, there will always be a 'barrio' with festivities.

Las Fiestas de la Paloma are the most famous, as La Virgin Paloma is one of the most famous saints of Madrid. It is always the week before the 15th, and the streets get filled with food and booze stalls, with activities and music.

People get dressed as chulapos and chulapas (with the typical Madrilenian attire) and have some lemonade (alcoholic). During the day they have some activities and theatre for kids, and during night time, concerts. The 15th is the day where they actually get the Virgin out on the streets, and they do a small parade with her around part of the city. And at the end, since this saint is the patron of the Firefighters, they usually do a show at Puerta de Toledo full of jumps, trucks and water spraying.

49. Parque Del Capricho, A Fancy Park

El Capricho Park is a bit far away from the center but absolutely worth it, as it is not as crowded, and it is just spectacular. It is at Paseo Alameda de Osuna, 25. There is a Metro stop called El Capricho, so you can't miss it.

It has a lake, a palace, and quite a few fountains. It was built in the 1700s and 1800s, so it has quite a French, Italian and English influence in its statues.

Almost all year round there are free guided visits, so try to make a reservation before you go if you want to do this (although the tickets go away... fast!)

50. Visit A Ghost Train Station

Madrid has a ghost train station, where trains still go through but do not stop. It's the Chamberi Metro station, between Bilbao and Iglesia at line 1 (light blue line).

If you want to go, you have to get off Bilbao or Iglesia and walk there to Luchana, 38-40.
There is a mini museum and a small documentary about the station. You can´t actually get in though, and there is a one person in, one person out policy, so be there early.

Ana Alonso

Top Reasons to Book This Trip

- **Food**: Madrid's food is fantastic: tapas and Spanish food will keep you full all the time!

  Hamburgers, bocadillos de calamares, churros and much more will be waiting for you.

- **Culture**: you will be able to see part of Spain's history through its buildings and museums.

- **Liveliness**: Madrid has something to do 24/7. The city does not stop. But if you need some peace, there is also places to be quiet.

Ana Alonso

> TOURIST

GREATER THAN A TOURIST

Visit GreaterThanATourist.com
http://GreaterThanATourist.com

Sign up for the Greater Than a Tourist Newsletter
http://eepurl.com/cxspyf

Follow us on Facebook:
https://www.facebook.com/GreaterThanATourist

Follow us on Pinterest:
http://pinterest.com/GreaterThanATourist

Follow us on Instagram:
http://Instagram.com/GreaterThanATourist

Ana Alonso

> TOURIST

GREATER THAN A TOURIST

Please leave your honest review of this book on Amazon and Goodreads. Thank you.

We appreciate your positive and negative feedback as we try to provide tourist guidance in their next trip from a local.

Our Story

Traveling is a passion of the "Greater than a Tourist" series creator. Lisa studied abroad in college, and for their honeymoon Lisa and her husband toured Europe. During her travels to Malta, an older man tried to give her some advice based on his own experience living on the island since he was a young boy. She was not sure if she should talk to the stranger but was interested in his advice. When traveling to some places she was wary to talk to locals because she was afraid that they weren't being genuine. Through her travels, Lisa learned how much locals had to share with tourists. Lisa created the "Greater Than a Tourist" book series to help connect people with locals. A topic that locals are very passionate about sharing.

Ana Alonso

Notes

Made in the USA
Coppell, TX
09 February 2023

About the Author

Dan Jorgensen is a native of Minnesota who grew up in South Dakota. A journalist and public relations practitioner, he has written many hundreds of journalistic articles and 7 books and taught both journalism and creative writing. His latest, the award-winning *And The Wind Whispered*, is out in paperback and all e-book formats. He and his wife Susan reside in Milliken, Colorado. They are the parents of two adult daughters, Kari and Becky, who each have families of their own.

Acknowledgements

The book is dedicated to Susan, my best friend...and best reader of my work.

Sincere thanks to Carolyn Amiet and Dr. Kelvin F. Kesler, M.D., F.A.C.O.G., for their help and advice in the construction of this book.

Also by Dan Jorgensen

Novels

And The Wind Whispered
Sky Hook
Andrea's Best Shot
Dawn's Diamond Defense
Kellie's Choice

Non-fiction

Family Hiking Trails of South Dakota
(With Roger Brandt)
Jargon – The Book

Play

The First Day

Anthology Inclusion

A Farm Family Christmas

Made in the USA
Thornton, CO
01/31/23 19:07:25

f58090b7-b5aa-4562-b73f-0225f7557574R01